# Howells

### by Iain Gray

WRITING *to* REMEMBER

WRITING *to* REMEMBER

79 Main Street, Newtongrange,
Midlothian EH22 4NA
Tel: 0131 344 0414
E-mail: info@lang-syne.co.uk
www.langsyneshop.co.uk

Design by Dorothy Meikle
Printed by Printwell Ltd
© Lang Syne Publishers Ltd 2022

All rights reserved. No part of this publication may be reproduced, stored or introduced into a retrieval system, or transmitted in any form or by any means (electronic, mechanical, photocopying, recording or otherwise) without the prior written permission of Lang Syne Publishers Ltd.

ISBN 978-1-85217-662-4

# Howells

**MOTTO:**
Virtue in difficulty.

**CRESTS** include:
A rose between two wings
and emerging from a ducal crown
(and)
Three castellated towers
(and)
A griffin holding a broken spear.

**NAME** variations include:
Hawell
Howel
Howell
Howels

*Chapter one:*

# Origins of Welsh surnames

by Iain Gray

***If you don't know where you came from, you won't know where you're going* is a frequently quoted observation and one that has a particular resonance today when there has been a marked upsurge in interest in genealogy, with increasing numbers of people curious to trace their family roots.**

Main sources for genealogical research include census returns and official records of births, marriages and deaths – and the key to unlocking the detail they contain is obviously a family surname, one that has been 'inherited' and passed from generation to generation.

No matter our station in life, we all have a surname – but it was not until about the middle of the fourteenth century that the practice of being identified by a particular, or 'fixed', surname became commonly established throughout the British Isles.

Previous to this, it was normal for a person to be identified through the use of only a forename.

Wales, however, known in the Welsh language as *Cymru*, is uniquely different – with the use of what are known as patronymic names continuing well into the fifteenth century and, in remote rural areas, up until the early nineteenth century.

Patronymic names are ones where a son takes his father's forename, or Christian name, as his surname.

Examples of patronymic names throughout the British Isles include 'Johnson', indicating 'son of John', while specifically in Scotland 'son of' was denoted by the prefix Mc or Mac – with 'MacDonald', for example, meaning 'son of Donald.'

Early Welsh law, known as *Cyfraith Hywel*, *The Law of Hywel*, introduced by Hywel the Good, who ruled from Prestatyn to Pembroke between 915 AD and 950 AD, stipulated that a person's name should indicate their ancestry – the name in effect being a type of 'family tree.'

This required the prefixes *ap* or *ab* – derived from *mab*, meaning 'son of' being placed before the person's baptismal name.

In the case of females, the suffixes *verch* or *ferch*, sometimes shortened to *vch* or *vz* would be attached to their Christian name to indicate 'daughter of.'

In some cases, rather than being known for

example as *Llewellyn ap Thomas* – *Llewellyn son of Thomas* – Llewellyn's name would incorporate an 'ancestral tree' going back much earlier than his father.

One source gives the example of *Llewellyn ap Thomas ap Dafydd ap Evan ap Owen ap John* – meaning *Llewellyn son of Thomas son of Dafydd son of Evan son of Owen son of John*.

This leads to great confusion, to say the least, when trying to trace a person's ancestry back to a particular family – with many people having the forenames, for example, of Llewellyn, Thomas, Owen or John.

The first Act of Union between Wales and England that took place in 1536 during the reign of Henry VIII required that all Welsh names be registered in an Anglicised form – with *Hywel*, for example, becoming Howell, or Powell, and *Gruffydd* becoming Griffiths.

An early historical example of this concerns William ap John Thomas, standard bearer to Henry VIII, who became William Jones.

In many cases – as in Davies and Williams – an s was simply added to the original patronymic name, while in other cases the prefix *ap* or *ab* was contracted to *p* or *b* to prefix the name – as in *ab Evan* to form Bevan and *ap Richard* to form Pritchard.

Other original Welsh surnames – such as Morgan, originally *Morcant* – derive from ancient Celtic sources, while others stem from a person's physical characteristics – as in *Gwyn* or *Wynne* a nickname for someone with fair hair, *Gough* or *Gooch* denoting someone with red hair or a ruddy complexion, *Gethin* indicating swarthy or ugly and *Lloyd* someone with brown or grey hair.

With many popular surnames found today in Wales being based on popular Christian names such as John, this means that what is known as the 'stock' or 'pool' of names is comparatively small compared to that of common surnames found in England, Scotland and Ireland.

This explains why, in a typical Welsh village or town with many bearers of a particular name not necessarily being related, they were differentiated by being known, for example, as 'Jones the butcher', 'Jones the teacher' and 'Jones the grocer.'

Another common practice, dating from about the nineteenth century, was to differentiate among families of the same name by prefixing it with the mother's surname or hyphenating the name.

The history of the origins and development of Welsh surnames is inextricably bound up with the nation's frequently turbulent history and its rich culture.

Speaking a Celtic language known as Brythonic, which would gradually evolve into Welsh, the natives were subjected to Roman invasion in 48 AD, and in the following centuries to invasion by the Anglo-Saxons, Vikings and Normans.

Under England's ruthless and ambitious Edward I, the nation was fortified with castles between 1276 and 1295 to keep the 'rebellious' natives in check – but this did not prevent a series of bloody uprisings against English rule that included, most notably, Owain Glyndŵr's rebellion in 1400.

Politically united with England through the first Act of Union in 1536, becoming part of the Kingdom of Great Britain in 1707 and part of the United Kingdom in 1801, it was in 1999 that *Cynulliad Cenedlaethol Cymru*, the National Assembly for Wales, was officially opened by the Queen.

Welsh language and literature has flourished throughout the nation's long history.

In what is known as the Heroic Age, early Welsh poets include the late sixth century Taliesin and Aneirin, author of *Y Gododdin*.

Discovered in a thirteenth century manuscript but thought to date from anywhere between the seventh and eleventh centuries, it refers to the kingdom of Gododdin that took in south-east Scotland and

Northumberland and was part of what was once the Welsh territory known as *Hen Ogledd*, *The Old North*.

Commemorating Gododdin warriors who were killed in battle against the Angles of Bernicia and Deira at Catraith in about 600 AD, the manuscript – known as *Llyfr Aneirin*, *Book of Aneirin* – is now in the precious care of Cardiff City Library.

Other important early works by Welsh poets include the fourteenth century *Red Book of Hergest*, now held in the Bodleian Library, Oxford, and the *White Book of Rhydderch*, kept in the National Library of Wales, Aberystwyth.

William Morgan's translation of the Bible into Welsh in 1588 is hailed as having played an important role in the advancement of the Welsh language, while in 1885 Dan Isaac Davies founded the first Welsh language society.

It was in 1856 that Evan James and his son James James composed the rousing Welsh national anthem *Hen Wlad Fynhadad – Land of My Fathers*, while in the twentieth century the poet Dylan Thomas gained international fame and acclaim with poems such as *Under Milk Wood*.

The nation's proud cultural heritage is also celebrated through *Eisteddfod Genedlaethol Cymru*, the National Eisteddfod of Wales, the annual festival of music, literature and performance that is held across the nation and which traces its roots back to 1176 when Rhys ap Gruffyd, who ruled the territory of Deheubarth from 1155 to 1197, hosted a magnificent festival of poetry and song at his court in Cardigan.

The 2011 census for Wales unfortunately shows that the number of people able to speak the language has declined from 20.8% of the population of just under 3.1 million in 2001 to 19% – but overall the nation's proud culture, reflected in its surnames, still flourishes.

Many Welsh families proudly boast the heraldic device known as a Coat of Arms, as featured on our front cover.

The central motif of the Coat of Arms would originally have been what was borne on the shield of a warrior to distinguish himself from others on the battlefield.

Not featured on the Coat of Arms, but highlighted on page three, is the family motto and related crest – with the latter frequently different from the central motif.

Echoes of a far distant past can still be found in our surnames and they can be borne with pride in commemoration of our forebears.

*Chapter two:*

# Illustrious pedigree

**A name of uniquely Welsh origin, 'Howells' and its equally popular spelling variant of 'Howell' derive from the forename 'Howell' or 'Howells', which in turn derive from the Welsh 'Hoel' or 'Hywel.'**

Of ancient roots and meaning "the eminent one" and with 'Howells' indicating 'son of Howell' and 'Howell' an Anglicisation of the Welsh form, the name features prominently in the frequently turbulent historical record.

In eastern England, meanwhile, the name is thought to have arrived through settlers from Brittany in the forms of 'Howael' or 'Hewel', while yet another possible point of origin is from the locational name of 'Howell' in the English county of Lincolnshire and derived from the Old English 'hugol', meaning 'hillock' or 'mound.'

One reason for the popularity of the forename from which the surname derives is that from throughout the Middle Ages it was proudly borne in honour of the great ninth century Welsh king and lawmaker Hywel Dda – Hywel the Good.

Hywel himself had an illustrious pedigree,

descended as he was from the famed Rhodri ap Merfyn, better known to posterity as Rhodri Mawr, or Rhodri the Great.

Born in about 820 and succeeding his father when he was aged 24 as King of Gwynedd, Rhodri came to control much of what is now modern-day Wales – to the extent that some sources refer to him as 'King of Wales.'

In what were particularly bloody times, he had to contend with both Saxon and Viking invasions – with the Vikings referred to by the Welsh as 'the black gentiles.'

The Welsh historical source known as the *Chronicle of the Princes* records Rhodri killing the Viking leader Gorm in 856 after the Norsemen had ravaged Anglesey.

Confusion surrounds the latter years of his kingship, with the chronicle stating that he was killed fighting the Vikings at 'the battle of Sunday' on Anglesey in 873, while other sources assert he was killed four years later along with his brother Gwriad in fierce battle with the Saxons.

His descendant Hywel Dda, also known as Hywel ap Cadell, born in about 880, was the king of Deheubarth and came to rule over the entire country from Prestatyn to Pembroke.

Of the noble Dinefwr branch of Rhodri the Great's Gwynedd dynasty, he was the son of Cadell, king of Seisyllwg, and married to Elen, heiress of Llywarch, king of Dyfed.

It was along with his brother Clydog that Hywel ruled Seisyllwg following the death of his father and, following Clydog's death in 920, he created the single realm of Deheubarth by uniting the kingdoms of Seisyllwg and Dyfed.

He became ruler of Gwynedd and also the kingdom of Powys by about 940, a vast territory and that explains why some sources such as the *Annales Cambriae – The Annals of Wales –* go so far as describing him as 'King of the Britons.'

He had gone on pilgrimage to Rome in 928, undertaking an intensive study of legal systems that included those of the Islamic world, and this had a profound influence on him when between 940 and 945, he codified the Welsh law that became known as as *Cyfraith Hywel*, *The Law of Hywel*.

These laws were revolutionary for their time in that, for example, they recognised the rights of women and allowed for protection of the weak while, as referred to in *Chapter one*, they also stipulated that a person's name should indicate their ancestry – the name in effect being a type of 'family tree.'

Hywel Dda died in 950, while the original home of the National Assembly for Wales, now a teaching centre that hosts young people's debates, is known as Tŷ Hywel – Hywel's House.

The death knell of Welsh independence was sounded in October of 1066 with the Norman Conquest of that year, when England's Anglo-Saxon monarch Harold II was defeated by a mighty invasion force led by Duke William II of Normandy that had landed at Hastings, in East Sussex.

Harold drew up a strong defensive position, at the top of Senlac Hill, building a shield wall to repel William's cavalry and infantry.

Although the Normans suffered heavy losses, they eventually won the day through a combination of the deadly skill of their archers and the ferocious determination of their cavalry.

Morale had collapsed on the battlefield as word spread through the ranks that Harold, the last in a long line of Anglo-Saxon kings, had been killed.

William was declared King of England on December 25, and the complete subjugation of his Anglo-Saxon subjects followed, with those Normans who had fought on his behalf rewarded with lands – a pattern that was repeated in Wales.

This subjugation is reflected in the famous

*Domesday Book*, a massive survey of much of England and Wales, ordered by William to determine who owned what, what it was worth and therefore how much they were liable to pay in taxes to the voracious Royal Exchequer.

Completed in 1086 and now held in the National Archives in Kew, London, 'Domesday' was an Old English word meaning 'Day of Judgement.'

This was because, in the words of one contemporary chronicler, "its decisions, like those of the Last Judgement, are unalterable."

It had been a requirement of all landholders – from the richest to the poorest – that they identify themselves for the purposes of the survey and for future reference by means of a surname.

This is why the *Domesday Book*, although written in Latin as was the practice for several centuries with both civic and ecclesiastical records, is an invaluable source for the early appearance of a wide range of surnames.

A Prince Hoel, is recorded in the *Domesday Book* as Prince of Caerlon-upon Usk, in Monmouthshire, and it is here that bearers of the Howells and Howell names are particularly associated.

One of the thirteen historic Welsh counties and known in Welsh as *Sir Fynwy* – with 'Sir' denoting 'county' – it is famous for landmarks that grace the landscape that include Raglan Castle, Abergavenny Castle and Tintern Abbey.

*Chapter three:*

# Religion and politics

**A descendant of Hywel Dda, Thomas Howell was the late sixteenth to mid-seventeenth century ecclesiastic born in 1588 in Llangamarch, Breconshire.**

Graduating from Jesus College, Oxford, in 1607 and subsequently ordained as a minister, he was appointed to the prestigious post of chaplain to Charles I and also as rector of the parish of Horsley in the English county of Surrey on the recommendation of the monarch.

The appointment of this 'outsider', however, provoked controversy among the parishioners, particularly because he haughtily refused to live in the parish.

He was appointed to the rectory of Fulham in 1642 – a key historical date because this was when the English Civil War was sparked off.

Charles I had incurred the wrath of Parliament by his insistence on the 'divine right' of monarchs, and added to this was Parliament's fear of Catholic 'subversion' against the state and the king's stubborn refusal to grant demands for religious and constitutional concessions.

Matters came to a head with the outbreak of the war, with Parliamentary forces, known as the New Model Army and commanded by Oliver Cromwell and Sir Thomas Fairfax, arrayed against the Royalist army of the king.

In what became an increasingly bloody and complex conflict, spreading to Scotland and Ireland and with rapidly shifting loyalties on both sides, the 49-year-old king was eventually captured and executed in January of 1649 on the orders of Parliament.

As the war had raged, Howell was hauled before the House of Commons and questioned over his loyalty to the ill-fated monarch and for having criticised Parliament.

But he managed to weather the storm and, in 1644, was appointed Bishop of Bristol – but only a year later and five years before his death in 1650, he was ejected from the bishopric after the Royalist forces that held the town surrendered to Sir Thomas Fairfax.

Also in the ecclesiastical realm, Rees Howells, born in 1879 in Brynaman, Carmarthenshire was the missionary noted for having founded the Welsh Bible College, in Swansea.

Immigrating to the United States in 1901 after having worked from the age of twelve in a tinplate mill, he found similar employment in Pennsylvania.

Returning to his home village of Brynaman in 1910 and marrying local woman Elizabeth Hannah Jones and having been influenced by an evangelist while in America, he enrolled in the Presbyterian College, Carmarthen.

Invited to become a missionary, both he and his wife joined the South African General Mission in 1915 – returning to their native land five years later.

After undertaking a preaching tour of America, in 1922 he resolved to establish a bible college in his native land to train missionaries.

Against all the odds managing to purchase the Glynderwen estate in Swansea, his Bible College opened in 1924.

Other estates – bought with the help of what Howells called "faith and prayers" – were acquired throughout the 1930s, enabling the establishment of a boarding school for the children of missionaries and also a small hospital.

Author of the 1940 *God Challenges the Dictators* – that uncannily prophesied in detail the end of the war in favour of the Allies and the ultimate fate of Nazi leader Adolf Hitler – he died in 1950.

In the often cut-throat world of politics, Geraint Wyn Howells was the Liberal Party politician, advocate for Welsh devolution, farmer and leading spokesman for agricultural interests born in 1925 in Brynglas, Ponterwyd, Cardiganshire.

Elected Member of Parliament (MP) for Cardiganshire in 1974, in his maiden speech in the House of Commons he passionately stated his desire for the devolution of political power from Westminster to Wales and the need for aid for Welsh agriculture.

Appointed by then Liberal Party leader Jeremy Thorpe as the party's spokesman on Wales he was appointed spokesman for both Wales and for agriculture under Thorpe's successor David Steel.

A supporter of the promotion of the Welsh language he, along with the Conservative Party MP for Denbighshire Geraine Morgan, also lobbied for Welsh language television programmes and, ultimately, a dedicated Welsh language channel.

Made a life peer in 1992 as Lord Geraint, of Ponterwyd in the County of Dyfed, he also served from 1971 to 1983 as vice-chairman of the British Wool Marketing Board and, from 1977 to 1987, as chairman of Wool Producers of Wales Ltd.

Also president for a time of the Royal Welsh Agricultural Society, he died in 2004, while the palliative care residence centre at Bronglais Hospital, Anglesey – and for which he helped to raise more than £1m for a scanner – was named Tŷ Geraint

Palliative Care Resource Centre when it opened in 2007.

Born in Birmingham in 1923, Denis Howell was the veteran Labour Party politician who served as MP from 1955 to 1959 for Birmingham All Saints and, from 1961 until his retirement in 1992, for Birmingham Small Heath.

Top ministerial posts that the keen cricketer and football referee held included, from 1969 to 1970, Minister for Housing and Local Government and, from 1974 to 1979, Minister for Sport and Recreation.

In 1974, his wife and son escaped injury when a bomb planted by the IRA exploded in their car on the driveway of their Birmingham home.

Rather odd posts he held include, during the particularly dry summer of 1976, Minister for Drought then, when the drought gave way to torrential rains, Minister of Floods – while during the severe winter of 1978/79 he was Minister of Snow.

Created a life peer in 1992 as Baron Howell of Aston Manor in the City of Birmingham and having published his memoir *Made in Birmingham*, he died in 1998.

Having held a number of Government ministerial posts, Kim Howells is the Welsh Labour Party politician who served from 1989 to 2010 as MP for Pontypridd.

Born in 1946 in Merthyr Tydfil, the son of a lorry driver, he studied history – gaining a PhD from the University of Warwick – before becoming an official of the South Wales National Union of Mineworkers (NUM) and also a local representative of the Communist Party of Great Britain.

Joining the Labour Party in 1982, he was active in South Wales for the NUM during the miners' strike of 1984 to 1985.

After becoming a presenter and writer for radio and television and working as a college lecturer, he entered the House of Commons and went on to hold posts that included Opposition spokesman on Trade and Industry and also Foreign Affairs and Development and Co-operation.

Ministerial posts included Parliamentary Under-Secretary of State at the Department for Education and Employment and Minister for the Middle East, in the Foreign and Commonwealth Office.

Known for his outspoken views, in 2002, as a junior minister at the Department of Culture, Media, Sport, he famously criticised the annual Turner Prize for Art by writing: "If this is the best British artists can produce then British art is lost. It is cold, conceptual bullshit..."

Appointed to the Privy Council in 2009 and

thereby taking the title of the Right Honourable Kim Howells, he stood down from Parliament at the 2010 general election.

A Labour member of the House of Lords, Rosalind Patricia-Anne Howells, more properly known as Baroness Howells of St David's, was born in 1931 in St David's on the island of Grenada.

The first black woman to sit on the Greater London Council's (GLC's) training board and having served as a community and equal opportunities worker, posts she has held include director of the Greenwich Racial Equality Council and vice-chair at the London Voluntary Services Council.

Born in 1936, David Howell, more properly known as Baron Howell of Guildford, is the veteran Conservative Party politician who was MP for Guildford from 1966 until his retirement in 1997.

Having held posts that include, from 1972 to 1974, Minister of State for Northern Ireland and, in 1979, Secretary of State for Energy and also leader of the Conservative Party in the House of Lords, he is the father of the biographer and novelist Frances Osborne, who married Conservative Party politician and Chancellor of the Exchequer George Osborne in 1998.

Her biographies include the 2004 *The Bolter*,

based on the life and times of her ancestor Indina Sackville and *Lilla's Feast* – the life and times of her paternal great-grandmother Lilla Eckford, who wrote a housekeeping and cookery book while in a Japanese internment camp during the Second World War.

*Chapter four:*
# On the world stage

**Bearers of the Howells name and its popular spelling variant of Howell have achieved recognition through a colourful range of endeavours and pursuits.**

One half of the Welsh folk band Paper Aeroplanes, **Sarah Howells** is the singer, songwriter and vocalist born in Pembrokeshire.

Along with co-writer and producer Richard Llewellyn, she has enjoyed success with best-selling albums that include the 2009 *The Day We Ran into the Sea*, the 2011 *We are Ghosts* and, from 2013, *Little Letters*.

A vocalist in the musical genre known as 'trance', she has also had success, in collaboration with fellow musician John O'Callaghan, with the single *Find Yourself* and also with the 2009 compilation album *A State of Trance*.

In the genres known as 'progressive house' and 'tech house', **Danny Howells** is the internationally renowned English DJ and record producer born in 1970 in Hastings.

Ranked at No. 10 in *DJ* magazine's Top 100 DJs poll, his work as a producer includes his 1999

*Nocturnal Frequencies* series of 'mix' albums and *Nubreed 002*.

In a decidedly different musical genre, **Gwynne Howell** is the acclaimed Welsh operatic bass born in 1938 in Gorseinon, Swansea.

Having studied at the Royal College of Music, London, he joined Sadler's Wells Theatre in 1968 and, two years later, the Royal Opera House.

Noted for his bass performances in a number of Wagner and Verdi operas, in 2010 he also had the role of Schigolch in a Metropolitan Opera production of composer Alban Berg's *Lulu*.

Overcoming early family financial problems and personal illness, **Herbert Norman Howells** went on to become a noted twentieth century English composer, organist and teacher.

Born in 1892 in Lydney, Gloucestershire, the youngest of six children and the son of a builder, decorator, painter and plumber who played the organ in his local church, he showed early promise as a musician.

His father taught him to play the organ, and he became deputy organist at a local Church of England church and one of its choirboys when aged 11.

Disaster struck the family when Howells was aged about 13 when his father was declared bankrupt – but a member of the family of Charles Bathurst, 1st

Viscount Bledisloe, who had been impressed by the musical prodigy, funded music lessons for him under Herbert Brewer, the organist of Gloucester Cathedral.

Aged 16 when he became a full-time pupil at the cathedral, one of his fellow pupils was the future composer and actor Ivor Novello.

Later studying at the Royal College of Music, London, where one of his fellow pupils was the future composer and conductor Arthur Bliss, Howells would become famous for his Anglican Church musical compositions.

He had his first composition, *Mass in the Dorian Mode*, performed while still a pupil in the hallowed confines of Westminster Cathedral.

By 1915, by which time he had also composed *Psalm Preludes*, he was struck by Graves' disease, which affects the thyroid, and given only six months to live.

But through regular injections over a two-year period of what was then the largely untried and untested treatment of radium injections, the condition abated.

Assistant organist for a time at Salisbury Cathedral and then employed to work with the choir at Westminster Cathedral, he continued to compose significant works that include his three carol anthems

*Here is the Little Dove*, *A Spotless Rose* and *Sing Lullaby*, his 1938 *Concerto for Strings* and *Hymnus Paradisi*.

Also a member of the teaching staff of the Royal College of Music until four years before his death in 1983 at the age of 91, he was the father of the stage, television and film actress **Ursula Howells**.

Born in 1925 and having done much to promote her later father's work through the Herbert Howells Society, her first stage appearance was in Dundee in 1939 in a production of *Bird in Hand*.

Having also performed in the West End and on Broadway, her film credits include the 1952 *I Believe in You*, the 1954 *The Weak and the Wicked* and the 1998 *The Tichborne Claimant*, while television credits include the role of Frances in *The Forsyte Saga*, *Miss Marple* and *Midsomer Murders*.

In the early Howells and Howell homeland of Wales, **Gerran Howell** is the actor born in 1991 in Barry, Vale of Glamorgan.

Best known for his role of Vladimir Dracula in the 2006 CBBC television series *Young Dracula*, his other television credits include the drama *The Sparticle Mystery* and *Casualty*.

Holder of the Miss USA title in 1958, **Arlene Howell** is the American actress born in 1939 in Delhi, Richland Parish, Louisiana.

Taking to the stage shortly after winning the Miss USA title and also being placed third in the Miss Universe contest, her television credits include *Maverick*, *Bronco*, *77 Sunset Strip* and *Gomer Pyle*.

Better known by his stage name of **C. Thomas Howell**, Christopher Thomas Howell is the American actor whose career began at the tender age of only four in an episode of television's *The Brian Keith Show*.

Also a child stunt performer the actor, born in 1966 in Van Nuys, California, has big screen credits that include the 1982 *E.T. the Extra-Terrestrial*, the 1983 *The Outsiders*, the 2012 *Red Dawn* and, also from 2012, *The Amazing Spider-Man*.

Dubbed "the scream of the screen" and "the girl Charlie Chaplin", **Alice Howell** was the American actress of the silent film era born in 1886 in New York City.

Working for a time for director Mack Sennett and later the L-KO Kompany, her many screen credits include the 1914 *Caught in a Cabaret*, the 1915 *Mabel and Fatty's Married Life* and the 1926 *Madame Dynamite*.

Having also appeared in the sound movie era in the 1933 *The Black Ace* – rather ironically with no lines because she played the role of a mute servant – she died in 1961.

Back on British shores, **Anthony Howell** is the English actor best known for his role of police sergeant Paul Milner in the *Foyle's War* television series that also stars Michael Kitchen and Honeysuckle Weeks.

Born in the Lake District in 1971, as a stage actor he has performed leading roles with the Royal Shakespeare Company – including that of Benvolio in *Romeo and Juliet* – while other television credits include the 1999 BBC series *Wives and Daughters* and the 2010 *Dirk Gently*.

In the highly competitive world of sport, **David Howells** is the English former midfielder who was on the winning Tottenham Hotspur side in the 1991 Cup Final against Nottingham Forest.

Born in 1967 in Guildford, he also played for Southampton and Bristol City before a knee problem forced his retirement from the game.

On the golf course, **Charles Howell III** is the American professional player who first took up the clubs when he was aged seven.

Born in 1979 in Atlanta, Georgia – home to the prestigious Masters Tournament – and turning professional in 2000, he has been ranked in the top 15 of the official World Golf Ranking.

From sport to the creative world of the written word, **William Dean Howells** was the American literary critic, playwright and author in the genre known as realism.

Born in 1837 in what is now Martin's Ferry, Ohio, the second of eight children, his father was a newspaper editor and printer – and from an early age the future author worked as a 'printer's devil', helping his father with typesetting and printing.

Aged only 15 when one of his poems was published in the *Ohio State Journal* – after having been submitted by his father without his knowledge – he later became editor of the *Atlantic Monthly*.

Known in his lifetime as "The Dean of American Letters", before his death in 1920 he wrote works that include the Christmas tale *Christmas Every Day*, the 1866 *Venetian Life*, the 1877 *A Counterfeit Presentment* and, from 1879, *The Lady of the Aroostook*.

From the written word to the equally creative world of architecture, **John Mead Howells** was the distinguished American architect born in 1868 in Cambridge, Massachusetts.

Having studied at Harvard University and the École des Beaux Arts in Paris, along with Isaac Newton Phelps – one of his fellow students in Paris – he founded the New York architectural firm of Howells & Stokes.

The two were responsible for works that

include Columbia University's magnificent St Paul's Chapel, while after the partnership was dissolved in 1913 Howells – greatly influenced by the Art Deco style and now in partnership with Raymond Hood – designed structures that still grace American cityscapes to this day such as the *Daily News* building in New York and the *Chicago Tribune* building.

Also responsible for the plan for the University of Brussels, in Belgium, his many awards and honours include election to the National Institute of Arts and the National Academy of Design and Officer of the Order of the Crown (Belgium).

The author of a number of books on architecture, he died in 1959.

Back on British shores and in the nineteenth century, one architect who had a rather unusual remit was **Charles Henry Howell**.

Born in London in 1824, he became the main architect in England during much of the Victorian era for lunatic asylums – as institutions for the mentally ill were then known.

Consultant architect to the Lunacy Commission and also surveyor of public buildings for the County of Surrey from 1860 to 1863, he died in 1905.